To the Top of Everest

Laurie Skreslet
with Elizabeth MacLeod

Kids Can Press

This story is dedicated to the memory of Blair Griffiths, Ang Chuldim, Dawa Dorje and Pasang Sona. It is also dedicated to my daughter, Natasha Skreslet, and all her generation of girls and boys who strive to be the best they can be!

Acknowledgments
I wish to give special acknowledgment to Valerie Hussey, who first invited me to put my story in print, and to Liz MacLeod, who worked with energy and insight. Thanks is given to the entire 1982 Canadian Mount Everest Expedition for contributing photos, and to Kids Can Press for publishing this personal journey to the top of the world. Some very special friends read the manuscript and offered wonderful ideas. For this I thank Colleen Campbell, Vicky Martins, Betsy McGregor, Baiba Morrow, Dave Pugliese and Sharon Wood. Finally — thanks, Glen, for being my friend!

Text © 2001 Laurie Skreslet

Kids Can Press acknowledges the financial support of the Ontario Arts Council, the Canada Council for the Arts and the Government of Canada, through the BPIDP, for our publishing activity.

Published in Canada by
Kids Can Press Ltd.
29 Birch Avenue
Toronto, ON M4V 1E2

Published in the U.S. by
Kids Can Press Ltd.
2250 Military Road
Tonawanda, NY 14150

www.kidscanpress.com

Edited by Charis Wahl
Designed by Julia Naimska

Printed and bound in Hong Kong by Book Art Inc., Toronto

This book is smyth sewn casebound.

CM 01 0 9 8 7 6 5 4 3 2 1

Canadian Cataloguing in Publication Data

Skreslet, Laurie
    To the top of Everest

ISBN 1-55074-721-5

1. Skreslet, Laurie. 2. Mountaineering — Everest, Mount (China and Nepal) — Juvenile literature.
3. Everest, Mount (China and Nepal) — Description and travel — Juvenile literature.
4. Mountaineers — Canada — Biography. I. Macleod, Elizabeth. II. Title.

GV199.44.E85S57 2001   j796.52'2'095496   C00-933215-4

Photo credits
Every reasonable effort has been made to trace ownership of and give accurate credit to copyrighted material.
Information that would enable the publisher to correct any discrepancies in future editions would be appreciated.
The 1982 Canadian Mount Everest Expedition: 5, 10, 16 (all), 17 (middle right), 27 (top left), 31 (bottom), 34 (top).
Tim Auger: 12–13. **Rusty Baillie:** 27 (middle right). **Carlos Buhler:** 7 (bottom), 9. **Calgary School Board:** 7 (top right).
Larry Derby: 4 (top). **Jeff Duenwald:** 55 (top). **Jim Elzinga:** 20 (top), 21 (left), 23 (top right), 54 (bottom). **Kurt Fuhrich:**
23 (middle left). **Lloyd Gallagher:** 51 (bottom). **Dan Griffith:** 8 (top). **Bill March:** 34 (bottom). **Dave McNabb:** 8 (bottom).
Morton Molyneux: 14 (both). **Pat Morrow:** 1, 3, 17 (bottom), 18 (top left), 20 (bottom), 22 (middle left), 23 (top left, top
middle, bottom), 24, 25 (both), 26 (both), 27 (top right), 28–29, 31 (top, middle), 32 (both), 33 (top), 37 (both), 38, 39, 41
(top), 43 (both), 46, 48, 49 (both), 50 (top). **Jim Muir:** 54 (top). **Bruce Patterson:** 52–53. **Jack Skreslet:** 6. **Laurie Skreslet:**
4 (bottom), 7 (top left), 11 (both), 15 (top and bottom right), 17 (top left), 18–19, 21 (right), 22 (top left, bottom left), 23
(middle right), 30, 33 (bottom), 35 (top, bottom), 36, 40 (middle), 41 (bottom), 42, 44, 45, 47, 50 (bottom), 51 (top), 55
(bottom). **Peter Spear:** 15 (top and bottom left). **Dave Read:** 40 (top).
Front cover photo: **Sharon Wood**
Back cover photo: **Laurie Skreslet**
Back flap photo: **Lloyd Gallagher**

Kids Can Press is a Nelvana company

Contents

Almost There ...

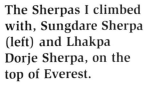

I'm Laurie Skreslet. This is my story of climbing Mount Everest.

"Careful," I said to myself. "Don't slip — it's a long way down." My climbing partners, Lhakpa Dorje Sherpa and Sungdare Sherpa, and I had left the South Col shortly after 4:00 in the morning on almost no rest or food — at heights like these, you feel too sick to sleep or eat.

And now, after years of preparation, 50 days of teamwork on the mountain and 5 exhausting hours of climbing, we were just below the summit of Mount Everest.

"Slowly. Take your time. Stay focused."

Carefully I stepped onto the summit, where Sungdare stood, but my foot broke through the snow's crust. I tried again — and again crashed through. So I plunged my ice ax into the snow, anchored it well, and pulled myself up. Lhakpa Dorje followed, and there we stood — on top of the world!

As I gazed around in awe, I thought about the rest of our team, far below, waiting for us to return. And of the four who would never hear of our victory — the four who had died on our climb.

Then I saw the faces of all the people who'd told me "You can't." You can't — it's too dangerous. You can't — you don't have enough experience.

But if I'd listened to them, I wouldn't be here, so high I could see the curve of the Earth!

The Sherpas I climbed with, Sungdare Sherpa (left) and Lhakpa Dorje Sherpa, on the top of Everest.

Mount Everest towers over the other mountains around it.

Growing Up

▲

Here I am with my mom when I'm about 4 years old. I hated dressing up!

When I was a kid, I would never have guessed I'd become a mountain climber. My father was very protective, maybe because I was an only child. But I grew up in Calgary, Alberta, and loved to hike in the nearby Rocky Mountains. There, I'd gaze up at the soaring ravens and wonder what it would be like to be high among the cliffs.

So did I head up to find out? Nope. My first climb was in the city — and looking back, it was a reckless thing to have done. But I was 9 years old, and when a friend challenged me to race him up the suspension cables of a bridge, I said, "Sure!" My friend yelled, "Go!" and the race was on. Or so I thought.

Partway up the cable, I looked to see where my friend was. He was nowhere in sight. Then I looked down. He was still on the ground.

"Hey! What happened to you?" I called.

"I changed my mind," he shouted back.

Great, I thought angrily, but the ground seemed farther away than the top, so I kept climbing.

Soon I got tired — and scared. Should I give up? My hands were so sweaty I could barely keep a firm grip on the cable.

When I looked down again, I saw that a crowd had gathered below. Then I heard someone say, "Stupid kid! I hope he falls."

What was his problem? Why would anyone want me to fall? It made me really angry — then totally determined to make it to the top. No way was some guy going to have the satisfaction of watching me fail.

Well, I made it — gasping and terrified — just in time to see the man walk away in disgust. I told myself then and there that I'd never give in to anyone who wanted to see me fail. Ever.

After that, I hiked in the mountains whenever I could. I did okay

in school, but a lot of it seemed to include learning to be like everyone else, not the person you wanted to be. Only the outdoors taught me that!

Climbing a 900 m (3000 ft.) pillar of granite during the 1970s in the Bugaboos, British Columbia.

When I was 14, I read about Outward Bound. Its motto is "To serve, to strive and not to yield," which sounded pretty good. This outdoor-education organization teaches about giving your best effort to reach a goal, about trying and trying until you succeed. And if you fail, they promise "You'll never be afraid to try again."

An Outward Bound course would be great — but I needed my father's permission and he was too concerned about my safety to give it. So I had to wait to fill my need for adventure until I was 17 and old enough to get a passport. Then, as soon as I could, I left home and became a merchant seaman. As I traveled the world as an apprentice engineer on cargo ships, I learned about engines and generators. I also discovered that the world wasn't as scary as I'd thought, because I could rely on myself to keep out — or get out — of trouble.

Me in Grade 8 — I sure don't look as if I enjoy school, do I?

Getting ready to climb a frozen waterfall when I was in my early twenties. Finally, I'm where I belong.

7

Learning to Climb

In spring 1970, when I was 20, I left the Merchant Marine and enrolled in the Colorado Outward Bound Mountain School. It would change the direction of my life.

I learned to rock climb safely, using proper techniques and equipment, and I also found out that I was pretty capable when I gave something my best effort. After the course ended, the school hired me for four months. I worked as an assistant to the assistant instructors, my first real job as a leader.

Outward Bound teaches you to picture the times you did your best and were successful, and to use these memories to encourage you to reach other goals. It also teaches that if you make a plan to reach a goal, and can understand and judge the risks, anything is possible.

In 1974, I became an instructor at the Canadian Outward Bound Mountain School, working four to eight months of the year. The rest of the time I worked on my climbing skills by mountaineering in North and South America.

Some people are natural climbers. They have good balance, aren't afraid of heights and can move smoothly and efficiently. Not me — I had poor balance, was afraid of heights and was clumsy. But I was

▲

Winter or summer — I climbed whenever possible. I still do!

▶

In 1981, I joined the Mount Everest Expedition for a climb on Nuptse, a mountain close to Everest. Right outside the tent door is a 900 m (3000 ft.) drop straight down!

8

determined and focused, and I performed better as things got tougher. Perhaps being able to handle more pain than others helped, too. As long as I stayed focused, experience would soon make up for my lack of natural ability.

About six years later, I started getting interested in the Canadian Mount Everest Expedition planned for 1982. I never dreamed of being part of it — after all, I'd had only ten years' high-altitude experience. Yet climbers I'd grown up with were on the team. Why not me? Because there was a nasty little voice inside me that said "You can't. You're not good enough. Forget it." That voice felt like a bully picking on me … and I don't like bullies.

So the next time I bumped into the team leader, George Kinnear, I asked him, "Are you still looking for climbers for your expedition?" I tried not to sound too eager.

"Why?" asked George. "Are you interested?"

"Well, sort of … I'm not sure."

"You're not? Then call me when you are," he said.

I called George that night.

I thought he would ask me if I had what it takes to get to the top. How could I know? But George just asked, "What can you contribute to the team?"

That was easy. Besides my climbing skills, I could offer other talents — I worked well as part of a team, knew a lot about climbing equipment, was a very good organizer and was totally committed to any project I undertook.

George invited me to meet the group so they could get to know me. I must have done okay because they decided that, as a tryout, I would go with them on a training climb on Nuptse, a mountain beside Mount Everest. That's how I found myself in Asia, beginning to get a sense of the team — and Everest's power.

The team worked smoothly together, and the climb went well. Upon our return to Canada, the team invited me to join the expedition. Me — Laurie Skreslet!

Almost at the top of a frozen waterfall. Brrr — cold and very wet.

The Mountain

You may know that Mount Everest is the tallest mountain in the world, but do you have any idea how huge it really is? Picture a mountain so big that it makes its own weather by changing the direction of clouds and wind.

Everest soars 8850 m (29 035 ft.) above the border of Nepal and Tibet. In Nepal the mountain is called Sagarmatha, which means "Head of the Sky," while Tibetans call it Chomolongma, or "Mother Goddess of the Earth." Westerners named the mountain after Sir George Everest, who was in charge of mapping the area in 1852. Until his team figured it out, no one had known exactly how tall the mountain was.

The first people to get to the top of Everest and back down safely were Sir Edmund Hillary and Tenzing Norgay Sherpa, in 1953. By 1982, when we climbed, people had tried to get to the top of Everest for 60 years. Only 129 of them had reached the summit. Sixty-seven had died trying, which means that, on average, of every three climbers who set out, only two returned alive.

Here's part of the reason why: As you climb, there's less and less oxygen in the air. Your body tries to adapt — climbers call this "acclimatizing" — but above 8000 m (26 250 ft.), it's almost impossible. Your head pounds, you can't eat, your joints ache, it's hard to concentrate, and you have no energy. Imagine playing a hard game of soccer with a really bad flu, and you'll have some idea of how climbers feel. But Everest isn't a game. If you make a mistake, you might die.

The west ridge and southwest face of Everest, the highest mountain in the world.

There were a number of routes our team could have taken to the top of Everest. We chose a tough one, up the right-hand side on the south face, known as the South Pillar. Why make something difficult even harder? Some people would say we were crazy. But we wanted to take a route that would challenge our mountaineering skills. Little did we know it would test far more than that.

For the Sherpa people, Everest is a live, sacred place. Any visitor can feel how special the mountain is. None of us talked about "conquering" Everest; we felt honored just to be on this amazing mountain. When you think of Everest as "Mother Goddess of the Earth," you go with respect for its power and leave your arrogance at home.

Getting to the summit wasn't really on my mind. There were a lot of great climbers on the team, and only a few of us would be chosen for the final push. So I figured that if I stayed focused and worked hard — by doing more than my best every day — I could be proud of being part of the team, no matter what happened.

Sherpas have amazing energy and strength.

SHERPAS

The people who live in the mountains near Everest are called Sherpas. Centuries ago, they came from Tibet. From living at the high altitude of the Himalayas for so long, they've developed extra red blood cells to carry more oxygen throughout their bodies. They carried equipment and supplies for early expeditions, but as they gained experience, they became excellent climbers, too. Today, Sherpanis, female Sherpas, perform the same mountain work the men do. Together, they operate successful climbing, trekking and tourism businesses.

Summit
8850 m (29 035 ft.)

Camp Four
7900 m (26 000 ft.)

South Col

Geneva
Spur

South
Face

Camp Two
6500 m (21 300 ft.)

Camp One
6000 m (19 700 ft.)

Khumbu
Icefall

Base Camp
5300 m (17 400 ft.)

Lhotse

Nuptse

Here are places on and around Everest that you're going to read about.

Camp Three
7000 m (23 000 ft.)

Western Cwm

Gear for the Climb

In 1977, the Canadian expedition applied for permission to climb the mountain. A permit was granted for 1982, which seemed a long time away, but a climb takes a lot of planning. During those five years, the team got together everything we'd need for the climb. More than 160 companies provided services, equipment, food and money — $3 million in all.

I'm good at working on details and have created some of my own climbing equipment. Because I've also modified gear to make it exactly right for a specific job, it was logical for me to help manufacturers be sure the hanging stoves, snow pickets (we used them to anchor our ropes into the snow), ladders (our bridges across the deep cracks in the ice called crevasses) and other equipment were perfect for our needs. I worked with the companies that manufactured our tents, sleeping bags and clothing, making certain that every item would keep us warm, dry and safe on Everest.

How? Well, our tents had to be light enough to carry, yet strong enough to stand up to high winds, falling rocks and heavy snow. We had to be able to set them up wearing our thick mitts, no matter how cold and tired we were, so they couldn't have any fiddly little bits.

Details are important when you're creating gear. Here I am discussing a few points with a tent designer.

A tent designer and I worked hard to create the best tents for the expedition.

Our sleeping bags and clothing had to be light but warm. The sleeping bags needed room at the bottom for our feet and water bottles. For sleeping high on Everest, we'd fill the bottles with boiling water and tuck them between our feet. The water bottles kept us warm for a few hours. (If we used them as pillows, they'd be frozen by morning.)

By the time we were ready to leave, we had 15.5 t (17 tn.) of gear.

The man in charge of organizing all the equipment was Peter Spear, who is a high school vice principal in Calgary when he isn't climbing mountains. Students at Peter's school worked long and hard packing our food for shipping to Nepal. All of it was carefully weighed, sealed in large plastic bags, and packed in boxes that were plastic lined and wax covered. On each box was a list of exactly what was inside. The boxes had to be watertight, because they'd be carried to Everest during the monsoon season, when it rained steadily for weeks.

The students packed dried soup (cans are too heavy), milk powder, sugar, tea, chocolate (lots of it!), pasta and precooked meals — such as spaghetti, omelettes and baked beans. The kids also snuck in encouraging notes, jokes and cartoons. Those notes really lifted our spirits when we found them on the mountain.

Thanks to Peter and the students, only one box of supplies was badly damaged on the way to Everest, despite the long, wet journey. What a great job they did.

High school students in Calgary spent hours packing food for us.

Our gear also included ice axes for climbing steep ice.

All of these boxes are only a small portion of our food.

This is an ice screw placed in solid ice. We used these to secure our ropes on Everest.

Heading to Everest

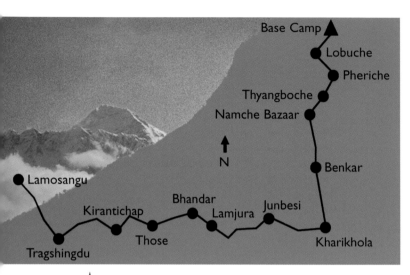

▲

Here's our route to Base Camp, at the foot of Everest.

Months before our climb, most of our equipment was flown from Canada to New Delhi, India. From there, four of us supervised its transport by truck, first to Kathmandu, the capital of Nepal, and then to Lamosangu, the closest a vehicle can get to Everest. From there, porters and yaks carried our cargo over 240 km (150 mi.) of trails to a village near Everest, then we returned to Canada.

The entire expedition except me left for Nepal mid-July 1982. (Some gear wasn't ready, so I volunteered to wait in Canada and bring it later.) On July 26, the team — 21 Canadians and 30 Sherpas — began the uphill trek from Lomosangu to Base Camp, at the foot of Everest. The 260 km (160 mi.) trek would help them get used to the thin mountain air.

Arriving later meant that I'd be trekking alone for a while, but that was okay: I'd trekked the route before. Besides, I wanted to think seriously about the climb ahead and why I was doing it. I needed that

►

Yaks are big — they can weigh 545 kg (1200 lb.) — but are nimble climbers.

Here are the boxes the students packed, on the way to Everest.

▼

16

time alone to harden my commitment and remove any remaining doubts. After all, on Everest, we were playing for keeps.

Spring and fall are the best times for climbing Everest. The bad news is that, to arrive at the right time in the fall, you have to trek to the mountain during the monsoon season. We slogged along trails turned to mud by rain. We were soaking wet, but we had to purify and carry our own drinking water. The streams looked clean, but were full of dangerous bacteria.

The most disgusting part was the leeches. These bloodsuckers would hang off trees overhanging the trail and drop on us. They'd lurk in the grass and cling to us as we passed. And they get all over you! Think of places you'd least like to find a leech, and we probably found one there — and they really hold tight. We had to sprinkle salt or iodine on the leeches to shrivel them up before we could pick them off.

For 7 days, I trekked for 14 hours a day and caught up with the team. Soon we'd left behind the forest (and leeches!) and were climbing through barren land. At a Tibetan Buddhist temple, we took

17

part in a sacred ceremony of protection for the Sherpas and us. The head lama gave us prayer scarves and sacred rice. We were to sprinkle the rice at especially dangerous places on Everest as a show of respect to the mountain spirits.

By the time we reached the last big village on our trek, we had climbed to 4500 m (14 800 ft.), higher than most peaks in the Rocky Mountains. The air was already so thin that my heart was pumping hard — I could feel it pounding in my throat.

Finally, on August 15, 1982, three weeks after the team had set out, we arrived in Base Camp. Now the challenge would really begin.

THE YETI

Sherpas believe the Yeti — what we call the Sasquatch or Abominable Snowman — is a humanlike creature that lives in mountains and deep forests. Other people think it's a rare type of bear that often stands on its hind legs, so it seems to walk upright like a person. It's hard to say, because few people have actually seen Yetis, but the Sherpas know those mountains best, so I figure they're right.

Pheriche is the last big village before Base Camp. We still had 750 m (2500 ft.) to climb to get to the foot of Mount Everest.

Life at Base Camp

Dave McNabb and I checked out the platforms for the tents we'd use high up on Everest.

Jim Elzinga (left) and Don Serl worked on our oxygen systems.

Peter Spear, the Base Camp manager, and a few others had arrived at Base Camp ahead of the team, and already had our tents up when we reached there. The tents had to be placed in a safe area, so the avalanches that roar down Everest almost every day wouldn't crush or bury the tents — or us!

There was still plenty for our team to do. All the equipment had to be unpacked and reorganized into the order it would be carried up the mountain. Every oxygen bottle had to be full and every piece of equipment checked. That included our crampons — sharp metal spikes attached to boots that dig into snow and ice and give secure footing.

It was also vital to check our ladders. They were light but strong enough to hold our weight when crossing crevasses. (Sometimes we'd bolt a few together when the crevasse was really wide.) The ladders had holes in the middle and ends so we could attach upright bars and string rope through them to make

handrails. Steel cables tensioned under the ladders kept them from sagging as we crossed.

Here are some ice screws and carabiners we used on Everest. Carabiners are the metal rings we used to attach our ropes to the ice screw.

It was hard to stay clean in Base Camp.

There was lots of other equipment to check. For instance, our climbing anchors. What are those? The team members climbing at the front of the group hammer in anchors — snow flukes, ice screws or snow pickets. A snow fluke is a metal plate with a steel wire in the center. It's buried in soft snow and holds the rope in place. An ice screw is used for hard ice and a snow picket for hard-packed snow.

The lead climbers string or "fix" rope through each anchor as they go. The anchors can be anywhere from 3 to 30 m (10 to 100 ft.) apart, depending on how hard the climbing is and what dangers have to be negotiated.

Once ropes are placed, other climbers follow, each carrying about 20 kg (45 lb.) of equipment. To make their ascent easier, climbers snap a Petzl ascender onto the ropes. This device also attaches to a climber's harness. If the climber slips, the ascender locks on the rope and stops him from falling. It slides up the rope easily but gives a climber a secure grip to pull on.

There was one piece of equipment I was very proud of — the butane/propane stoves we'd use to melt snow for drinking water (you can see one on page 33). On Everest, there's little flat ground for setting up a stove. So I created a stove that would hang from a tent ceiling. No matter what angle the tent was at, the stove stayed level — and the water didn't spill.

HELLO FROM MOUNT EVEREST

A mail runner arrived in Base Camp every five days with a huge bag crammed full of letters from friends and strangers, all wishing us luck. Videotapes were raced from the mountain by mail runners and helicopters to a TV studio in Kathmandu — 360 km (225 mi.) away. From there, a satellite relay bounced the signal between Earth and a satellite three times as it traveled to Canada.

When the first climbers summited in 1953, it took days for the news to get out. If any of us got to the top, we'd be able to let the world know in an hour.

Who's Who on the Team

Pat Morrow

Lloyd "Kiwi" Gallagher

Rusty Baillie

I had climbed with many of the guys on our training climb on Nuptse, but on Everest, I really got to know them.

I'd already spent a night with John Amatt in a blisteringly cold refrigerator truck. It sounds crazy, but John had set it up to test our cold-weather gear and to get people talking about the expedition. John was the expedition's business manager — he found sponsors to donate money or equipment (and made sure the public heard about their generosity).

So, one evening, for the 6:00 news, John, a news reporter and I climbed into this freezing cold truck to stay the night. Well, by midnight the reporter was so cold that he had to get out. When John and I emerged the next morning, we were surrounded by reporters.

"How do you feel?" they asked. "Are you all right?"

"Best rest we've had in weeks," I told them. "No phones to wake us!"

Who else was in Base Camp? Alan Burgess was one of the strongest climbers — if anyone made it to Everest's top, we figured it would be Alan. Tim Auger, James Blench, Dwayne Congdon, Jim Elzinga, Dave McNabb, Don Serl and Gordon "Speedy" Smith were also skilled climbers. Pat Morrow was an excellent climber and photographer. The expedition's official photographer and videographer was Blair Griffiths.

Climber Dave Read had a great sense of humor. I didn't know him well, but we became good friends by the end of the climb. A generous act by Dave near the top of Everest would change my life.

Then there was Rusty Baillie — his great spirit reflects the joy and passion mountains symbolize. Every morning in Base Camp, Rusty practiced tai chi. And while the team had slogged through the mud on its trek to Base Camp, Rusty jumped in every puddle — because he wasn't allowed to puddlejump when he was a kid!

I've already told you about Peter Spear, the Base Camp manager who worked so hard with his students to pack our food. What a great guy to have on the team — always cheerful. Peter worked in Base Camp and carried gear to Camp One. So did the cook, Kurt Fuhrich, and writer Bruce Patterson. Our doctors, Stephen Bezruchka and David Jones, also did some climbing and carried equipment.

I felt great respect and loyalty for Bill March. He'd replaced George

Dwayne Congdon

Alan Burgess (left) and Gordon "Speedy" Smith

John Amatt (left) and Blair Griffiths

Kinnear as the team's leader after George developed high-altitude illness climbing in the Andes. (He later recuperated.) Bill was a fine climber and a strong, capable expedition leader. Our deputy leader was Lloyd Gallagher — we called him Kiwi because of his heavy New Zealand accent. He had a great sense of humor and was responsible, supportive and very experienced in the mountains.

Bill March, me, Dave Read (left to right)

Dave MacNabb, Peter Spear, Jim Elzinga (left to right)

Here's most of the team. Altogether there were 21 Canadians, 30 Sherpas and additional staff.

So, that was our team. We had a lot of experience and many different skills. Soon we would be putting all of them to work. Did we have what it takes to get to the top? By August 18, it was time to leave Base Camp and find out.

Climbing an Icefall

This was the deepest, scariest crevasse of the climb. The first time I crossed it, I was on my hands and knees.

The most dangerous part of our route wasn't at the top, but right near Base Camp. The Khumbu Icefall is part of the glacier that flows down Everest. Strewn around are blocks of ice the size of large houses. The drop is not only almost straight down, but deep crevasses snake through it. Every day avalanches roar down the slope, and seracs — towers of ice as high as 45 m (150 ft.) — collapse without warning.

On August 18, about 2:00 A.M., four "fixers," including me, set out through the Icefall. We left at night because it's coldest then, and the colder the glacier is, the less it moves. As well as fixing line, we had to bridge the crevasses. Some were more than 90 m (300 ft.) deep. We took turns rappelling down the near side of each crevasse until the gap was narrow enough

DISAPPEARING INTO THIN AIR

Even at Camp One, the air is so thin that we got exhausted quickly. You see, it takes time for blood to develop extra red blood cells to trap what little oxygen there is at high altitudes and send it around your body. The thin air also lets the sun's rays blaze through. With no shade, we were sweltering and sunburned. Even before noon, the temperature at Camp One soared to 38°C (100°F).

to cross. Then we climbed up the far side to the surface. The team threaded ropes through verticals and lowered the ladder — or a couple of ladders bolted end to end — toward the climber on the other side. The team then worked from both sides to position the ladders safely.

Crossing a crevasse is scary because the ladders sag in the middle and it's a long fall to the bottom. We moved carefully but quickly and fixed rope through the Icefall in three days. Camp One was set up at 6000 m (19 700 ft.). We all carried gear to the camp along the route we had fixed. Usually, we'd arrive by mid-morning. We'd unload our packs and cover the gear with tarps. As soon as we could, we'd head back to Base Camp, where there was more oxygen in the air.

We'd spend four days carrying and then take a day off. In the 23 days it took to haul everything to Camp One, we developed enough red blood cells to press on to Camp Two.

▲

It was safer to climb the Icefall at night, but the darkness made it tough to see all the dangers that surrounded us.

◀

Carrying a ladder across another ladder was very awkward and difficult.

25

Disaster Strikes

Early on the morning of August 31 — a rest day for me — Rusty Baillie, Blair Griffiths, Pat Morrow, Peter Spear and a number of Sherpas were carrying through the Icefall. Suddenly, an avalanche broke loose 900 m (3000 ft.) above the climbers, ripping out the rope anchors and swinging Pat into the wall of snow as it roared down the mountain. Blair and the Sherpas near him were knocked down and shaken, but all of them were able to take care of themselves. Rusty was pushed down the mountain by the snow and almost buried. Luckily, one of the Sherpas was able to help him dig out.

Peter was completely buried except for one foot, which stuck out enough that Rusty and a Sherpa could pull him free, gasping for breath.

But where were Sherpas Pasang Sona, Ang Chuldim and Dawa Dorje?

A radio call came into Base Camp: emergency in the Icefall! We geared up and set off as fast as we could.

▲

We'd had so many successful carries through the Icefall that we'd almost lost sight of how dangerous it could be. Our reminder was sudden — and tragic.

▶

Removing Pasang Sona's body from the Icefall.

Blair Griffiths

One of the four chortens, or memorials, we erected for the men who were killed.

We eventually found Pasang Sona in the Icefall. We tried desperately to revive him but finally had to accept that he was dead — we carried his body to Base Camp. We never found Ang Chuldim or Dawa Dorje. Their bodies still lie under the snow of Everest.

But the Icefall wasn't finished with us. Three days after the deaths, some of us were carrying gear up from Base Camp. Blair, Dave Read, Rusty, Psang Tenzing Sherpa and Nima Tshering Sherpa were repairing a bridge in the Icefall. Suddenly, bang! An ice tower collapsed. Then other seracs began falling all around. Rusty and one of the Sherpas scrambled to safety over the crumbling towers.

Dave and another Sherpa were tossed into a crevasse. Luckily, the huge blocks of ice crashing down jammed together and formed a protective roof over them, keeping the snow from burying them. Rusty and a Sherpa helped them both out.

But Blair was pinned to the ice by a falling serac and killed instantly.

We radioed the tragic news to the rest of the team. The reply from Bill March, the team leader, was clear. Early the next morning, we were to remove the entire team from the mountain and descend to Base Camp.

Bill sensibly told us to leave Blair's body — he didn't want anyone injured attempting to retrieve it. But Bill didn't know that Blair was visible, so we couldn't just leave him there. We took the chance and brought Blair's body to Base Camp. A few days later, we cremated him during a very moving ceremony.

AVALANCHE!

Avalanches sweep down Everest's west shoulder almost daily, particularly after a snowfall. There's never much warning. First, you hear a loud crack, like a gunshot. Then, a thundering roar as the snow starts to move. The wind alone can knock you over. Avalanche sounds carry great distances on Everest, so it's easy to make a fatal mistake and think the avalanche is farther away than it is.

Some of the seracs were huge. I was terrified every time I had to make a carry past this one. ◄

Down the Mountain

Moving down through the Icefall was especially terrifying after the four deaths.

When Bill March ordered us to leave Camp One for Base Camp, he told Jim Elzinga and me to set out ahead and repair the Icefall so the others could descend safely. Jim and I replaced broken ladders and ropes and were about to head to Base Camp when I saw some of the others still above us.

The sight reminded me of a climb I had made in the Rockies. My partner had descended quickly, leaving me farther and farther behind in a dangerous section. I remembered how abandoned and vulnerable I felt — and angry that my partner hadn't waited for me. When I got down that mountain, I vowed I would never do that to a fellow climber, no matter what.

So I waited for the last climbers and we headed down together. As we crossed a crevasse, one of the Sherpas got the bridge's anchor rope tangled on his pack. He couldn't unhook the rope and was frightened, so I climbed out to help him. But just as I freed the rope, he turned and accidentally knocked me into the crevasse.

I thudded to a stop 6 m (20 ft.) below on an ice block that had fallen into the crevasse. The shock of landing knocked the breath out of me, but I knew how lucky I was. Far above me, I watched the horrified looks on the other climbers' faces change to relief when they saw that I was still moving.

The team quickly lowered a rope, which I clipped to my harness. I'd hit my chest on a sharp corner of ice, so each yank on the rope and every breath was incredibly painful. When I finally made it to the top of the crevasse, the other climbers lightened my pack, and two of the Sherpas helped me through the Icefall to Base Camp. The camp doctor bandaged my broken ribs, and I collapsed in my tent.

We used both aluminum and rope ladders to climb through the Icefall. ◀

We'd lost so much gear in the avalanche that we had to discuss whether we could go on. ▼

By this time, the weather had turned ugly. High winds and blowing snow kept us from climbing. Stuck in our Base Camp tents day after day, with little to think about except the endless storms and the deaths of our team-mates, some climbers decided to leave the expedition. One-third of the Canadians headed home, and two-thirds of the Sherpas refused to continue the climb. Our expedition, they said, had been infected with bad luck.

After two long weeks, the weather cleared, just in time for my bandages to come off. But I still couldn't breathe properly. The doctor told me I must get an X-ray — easy to say, but the nearest X-ray machine was at the hospital in Kunde.

I loaded my pack and headed off.

Four days later, I made it to the hospital — only to find that the X-ray machine was broken. Had my trek been a waste of time?

No — it had made me healthier. On my way to Kunde, I'd been breathing air with more and more oxygen and eating fresh, nutritious food instead of expedition rations. Because I wasn't at high altitude, I was healing much faster and suffering less physical breakdown than my teammates. Broken ribs or not, I was feeling stronger.

What now?

I headed back to Base Camp.

▲ Dave Read helped me remove the bandages from my ribs.

Back on Everest

While I was trekking down to Kunde, the rest of the team began climbing up through the Icefall again.

Alan Burgess, Pat Morrow and Speedy Smith took on the treacherous and exhausting job of breaking trail through the heavy snow. During the two weeks of storms, nobody had been able to maintain the fixed ropes that marked the trail — the climbers couldn't assume the ropes could be depended on to hold their weight. Every anchor and rope had to be checked, and many had to be refixed or replaced.

And the ladders we'd so carefully placed over the crevasses? The glacier had twisted some completely out of shape. Others had been pushed far out of position or had dropped to the bottom of crevasses. The team had to fish them out, dangling their ice picks from one end of long ropes, hooking the ladders and hauling them to the surface ... very carefully.

The constantly moving glacier damaged our bridges daily. We often had to retrieve (left) or re-anchor (right) bridges that the glacier had shifted.

There were emotional hurdles, too. Every trip out from Base Camp meant passing the fallen ice tower where Blair had died and the place where the bodies of the two Sherpas still lay. Each time, the climbers had to face a harsh truth — it was easy to die on Everest. By staying focused and alert and by working together, they could make the climb a little safer and less scary.

Within a week, Alan, Pat and Speedy had finished refixing the rope up the Western Cwm (you say it Coom — it's Welsh for valley) to the site for Camp Two. Then other climbers carried supplies to the camp. Despite the snow and high winds, it was exhilarating. Until now, they'd seen only partial views of the mountain, but from Camp Two the team could clearly see the route to the top. The summit loomed large and intimidating.

Bill March, Dave Read, Dwayne Congdon and Kiwi Gallagher were at Camp One when Bill decided to close the Icefall. He felt it was too dangerous to carry through anymore. This meant no one was allowed to climb up from Base Camp.

With the Icefall closed, the climbers would be completely on their own — and I'd be on the wrong side of the closed Icefall.

▲ Our ropes and ladders through the Khumbu Icefall were all in chaos after the avalanche.

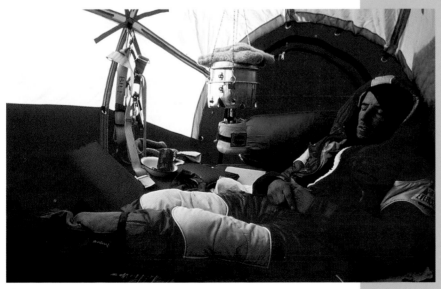

▲ Climbing all day was exhausting. Then we had to melt snow for hours to make enough water to drink.

WHAT'S FOR DINNER?

When you're climbing Everest, eating isn't very pleasant. Altitude sickness makes you feel as if you've got a really bad flu, and you have little appetite. Your nose is so stuffed up that you have to breathe through your mouth. Then, on the glacier, the bright sunshine reflects off the snow — right into your open mouth. It's not long before your tongue and the roof of your mouth are sunburned. Then every bite of food is agony.

We ate oatmeal, soup, tuna, crackers, chocolate bars, peanuts, raisins, tea, cocoa and coffee. But we especially loved our foil pouches of sliced peaches. By keeping them warm inside our jackets, the peaches slipped easily down our throats. And we drank lots of water. The weather's so cold and there's so little moisture in the air on Everest that you need up to 8 L (2 gal.) a day to keep from drying out.

Going It Alone

▲ This is one of the Icefall's crevasses that I had to cross. When we originally placed this ladder it was level. The glacier raised one side of the crevasse more than 15 m (50 ft.)!

▶ I had to think clearly as I moved through the Icefall — it was extremely dangerous. (The stuff on my face is protective zinc oxide.)

When I arrived back at Base Camp from Kunde, I was told the Icefall had been closed. I couldn't go through? Well, maybe — maybe not. I radioed Bill.

"Laurie, it's too dangerous. Stay in Base Camp!" Bill barked. "Do NOT —"

I flicked off the radio. That wasn't what I wanted to hear. After a year and a half of working on this expedition, I had too much energy invested to sit at the bottom of Everest. I'd gained a lot of experience in my years of climbing. I knew I could make an important contribution to the climbers struggling high on the mountain. It would all be wasted if I waited in Base Camp. So I took the risk.

Next morning I shouldered my pack and set off. Base Camp had radioed Bill, and he did the only thing he could — he ordered that no one come with me. Bill also insisted that I radio Base Camp every time I crossed a crevasse. If I fell, I was still on my own — the radio call would just let them know where to find my body.

At first, the climb wasn't too bad — I'd done it many times before, and with a heavier pack. The route was in much worse shape than my last time there, three weeks before, but most ladders were usable. The Icefall was quiet and the wind light.

Then I came to a crevasse about 3.5 m (12 ft.) wide. There was a ladder across it, but the ice had shifted since it had been put in place. Now the bridge ended 1.5 m (5 ft.) from the far wall. On my side, the end of the ladder was frozen into

the ice, but the other end hung 30 m (100 ft.) above the bottom of the crevasse.

No problem, I thought, I'll just find another place to cross.

For more than an hour, I searched desperately, but there was no other place. I had to admit defeat. Slowly, I started down to Base Camp.

Then I stopped. Did you give that your best? I asked myself.

Yes, I thought. But then I asked, Did you give it *more* than your best?

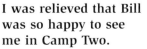
This is what Camp One looked like as I headed up to Camp Two.

No, I had to answer. More than my best was to go back and jump from the ladder to the far side. I knew the impossible is often the untried. I couldn't leave without trying, so back I went.

I decided to use the handrail ropes that were still there, adding new anchors and Petzl ascenders pointing both forward and back. I figured I had a fifty–fifty chance of making it across.

The ladder bobbed up and down as I edged my way out. At the end of the ladder, I focused all my concentration — and jumped.

Thwack! My ice pick bit into the ice on the lip of the crevasse. It held. I dug my crampons into the icy wall and used all my strength to pull myself up.

As I lay gasping on the far side, I realized that something powerful had happened. I seemed to be seeing things differently — everything was clearer and colors more vivid. It was like a different world. In making that leap, I'd let go not only of the ladder, but of some of my fears, too. I knew then that things would work out for me as long as I kept giving more than my best.

As I climbed to Camp One and on toward Camp Two, I thought about Bill. What would happen when I had to explain face-to-face why I'd disobeyed his order to stay in Base Camp? Would he allow me to keep climbing?

He was right there when I arrived.

"Laurie!" Bill shouted. Then he smiled and said, "It's great you're here!"

"Huh?" I said, stunned by his good humor.

"Look," said Bill, "four people have died. If I'd asked you to come up and something had happened to you, I couldn't bear to have another death on my conscience. I had to tell you to stay put." Bill paused. "But I knew you'd come up no matter what. So, welcome. I need you here."

I was relieved that Bill was so happy to see me in Camp Two.

35

Life on the Mountain

Closing the Icefall and cutting ourselves off from Base Camp forced the team to rethink the entire expedition. We had 8 Canadians, 12 Sherpas, a cookboy and more than one-third of our supplies at Camp One. That wasn't enough to make it up the South Pillar, as we had planned. But it was enough to get some climbers to the summit — if we switched to a less difficult route. Perhaps we'd been arrogant in our original, tougher choice.

Earlier in Base Camp, before I headed to hospital, the team had already decided to switch to the Southeast Ridge route. It would take us through an area called the South Col — a pass between Everest and Lhotse (a nearby mountain) — and then to the top.

We carried load after load up to Camp Two through brutally cold weather, high winds, driving snow and air that got thinner the higher

This is what we saw when we looked down the Western Cwm from Camp Two.

▼

Lhakpa Dorje and I digging out a tent at Camp Three after a night there.

It could be incredibly windy and snowy at Camp Three.

we went. Our routine went like this: First we'd carry loads to Camp Two for eight to ten hours. Then we'd melt snow and ice for three or four hours to make enough drinking water to replace all the liquid our bodies had lost that day in the cold, dry air.

A few days after we arrived in Camp Two, we began moving up the mountain to establish Camp Three. We set up camp at the base of the Geneva Spur on the Lhotse face, at about 7000 m (23 000 ft.).

For most of the climbers, sleep was difficult at Camp Three. The screaming wind lifted ice off the face of the mountain and sent it whizzing by us. In the morning, we'd often open the doors of our tents and see only a wall of snow. We had to keep shovels in the tents so we could dig ourselves out. It was so cold that even with bottles of hot water in our sleeping bags, we still had to wear all our clothes in the sleeping bags, sometimes even down parkas.

We were exhausted and often in pain, yet there was a powerful change in the group's spirit. During the first half of the climb, we'd worked well enough together, but personal differences and competitiveness had got in the way. Above the Icefall — after the tragedies — we had put our differences aside and become a real team.

GOING TO THE BATHROOM

Like most things on Everest, going to the bathroom can be a bit complicated. The main problem is that you're wearing a one-piece climbing suit — if you took it off, you'd freeze. So the suits are designed to get around that difficulty. A zipper runs down the front of the suit, between your legs and up your back to the middle of your shoulder blades. When fully open, the suit allows you to do your business, no problem — unless you get knocked over by wind or snow. Then you're in a real mess. I know because it happened to me. But only once. Yuck!

Getting There

Lhakpa Tshering Sherpa climbing above Camp Three.

▶

The wind could make it almost impossible to erect tents at Camp Three. We had to work as a team to accomplish this.

Slowly, carefully, we fixed rope above Camp Three and worked our way up the Geneva Spur. When avalanches ripped out our work, we started again. By September 30, Dwayne Congdon, Speedy Smith and two Sherpas had fixed rope up to 7770 m (25 500 ft.) — only about 1065 m (3500 ft.) from the summit. But the howling wind tore at the ropes and almost blew the climbers off the mountain.

The work was made even more dangerous because of our equipment. We had put on goggles to protect our eyes from the blinding sun. Some of us were also using oxygen because the air was so thin. But when we were wearing both goggles and an oxygen mask, it was difficult to see our feet — or where we were putting them.

Added to that, we were carrying coils of rope and had heavy bottles of oxygen strapped to our backs. But there was work to be done — we needed all our strength to place anchors in the ice, fix the rope and move gear up the slope.

Everest was dangerous even when we weren't climbing. One night, when everyone was in the tents at Camp Three, I decided to get more bottles of oxygen from the supply tent. It was only 6 m (20 ft.) away and I'd be outside only for a few minutes, so I didn't bother strapping on my crampons. I hadn't realized the snow was so hard that the edges of my boots wouldn't bite into it.

I lost my footing.

Fortunately, I had clipped my harness to the rope running between the tents. If I hadn't, I would have slid down the mountain and died from my injuries.

Clipping onto that rope had saved my life — and reminded me that, on Everest, one small mistake could be the last mistake I ever made.

EVEREST'S ANGEL

Late one night at Camp Two, I looked out of my tent. The night was so clear and beautiful that I went outside to see it better. Clouds were forming and reforming far down in the valley, heading toward me, and going straight up into the air. As I watched, the clouds slowly took the shape of an angel with outstretched arms. It hung in the sky as I stared in awe. As the angel faded away, I wondered what it meant. It seemed to be a sign that our expedition had a guardian angel that would protect us from further harm.

That night, I had my best sleep ever on Everest.

The Weather Closes In

Raging wind strong enough to blow a climber off his feet was making the situation so dangerous that we retreated to Camp Two. There, we huddled in our tents for two days, sick, cold and anxious — and thinking seriously about whether we should continue the climb.

For more than three weeks, we'd been at an altitude of over 6400 m (21 000 ft.), and it showed. Every part of our bodies ached, our lips were cracked, our fingertips and nails were shredded, and our noses bled all the time.

We sat tight in our tents while the winds stormed around us.

Some of the climbers suggested we go back to Base Camp to recuperate and wait out the storm. But I told Kiwi, our deputy leader, that I felt strong enough to keep carrying up to Camp Three — I'd much rather do that than go back down. Dave Read and Kiwi said they'd stay, too, and eventually everyone did. We were all worn out, but it felt right to keep on trying as long as we could.

Alan Burgess, Sungdare and Lhakpa Dorje braved the winds and fixed the rope up to the South Col. Overnight the weather improved, and we planned to make the best of it, for as long as it lasted.

We decided that a small group of climbers would climb from Camp Two to Camp Four in one day. Then, if the weather held, they'd

go for the summit. Bill chose Dave Read, Kiwi, me and seven Sherpas, including Sungdare and Lhakpa Dorje, to establish Camp Four. If that went well, we'd try for the top.

I wanted to see how high I could climb without oxygen, but Bill told me that I would help the expedition most by trying to climb to the summit as quickly as possible. That meant using oxygen. Bill wanted me to concentrate on the team's goals, not just my own. And he was right.

I stayed up late on the night of October 3, getting my equipment ready and concentrating on our immediate goal — establishing Camp Four, not reaching the summit. After all, anything could happen between here and there. Four deaths had already proved that.

From Camp Three, the summit of Everest towered above us.

41

We Head for Camp Four

Sleep was almost impossible that night. The thin air, constant nausea, bitter wind and excitement kept me awake. At 4:00 A.M. on October 4, Dave, Kiwi, seven Sherpas and I left Camp Two. The Sherpas and I reached Camp Three about four and a half hours later. I grabbed an oxygen bottle and breathing apparatus and kept going. Dave and Kiwi were moving more slowly and would catch up with us later.

I had a lot of trouble getting that oxygen mask to work — I'd never used one before — but the oxygen gave me a real boost. Despite the cold and wind, Sungdare, Lhakpa Dorje and I made great time, reaching the South Col about noon. When the other Sherpas arrived, we set up Camp Four, then they headed back to Camp Two at 2:30 P.M. Sungdare, Lhakpa Dorje and I crawled into a tent and melted snow and ice for the next four and a half hours. None of us had much appetite, so we just gulped down hot fluids.

Climbing to the top of the Geneva Spur, just below the South Col, was exhausting, even with oxygen.

We figured Dave and Kiwi had turned back to Camp Two. So we put in a radio call to check it out.

I was surprised to hear "Laurie, have Dave and Kiwi arrived?"

"Negative," I answered, feeling even colder. Where were they? We had no idea, but we had to find them. On went our gear, and we set off to search.

It was -44°C (-47°F), with the wind howling at around 80 km/h (50 m.p.h.). After an hour, we located Dave. His oxygen had run out, so we helped him to Camp Four, gave him oxygen and hot tea, and packed him into a sleeping bag. I radioed Bill, who told me to stay with Dave while the Sherpas searched for Kiwi.

The two Sherpas headed down, scanning the blackness for signs of life. Then the radio crackled again. Kiwi was safe at Camp Three. His oxygen equipment had failed and he'd turned around. We quickly radioed a message to the Sherpas to return to Camp Four.

After dealing with the emergency, we had only enough oxygen for three of us to try to summit the next day. Dave graciously volunteered to remain behind, suggesting that the two Sherpas and I would make the strongest team. His unselfish act put me in a position to be the first Canadian to summit Everest. For this and his great friendship, I am eternally grateful.

▲
At Camp Four there was lots of garbage from all the expeditions that had already used this site.

▼ **We established Camp Four high on the South Col, the windiest and coldest camp of all.**

DEALING WITH FEAR

On my first serious rock climb, back in 1971, my partner and I got trapped by a violent electrical storm halfway up a 300 m (1000 ft.) rock face. I was leading because my partner had been injured. I clung to the steep, wet, snow-covered rock, terrified. Climbing higher seemed impossible. So did climbing down. Frozen and scared, I started to cry.

I knew that even if all I did was hang on, I would eventually become so weak I'd fall. Then I realized that if I was likely to fall anyway, I'd rather be trying to climb out of there, not just standing there afraid. I chose to commit to action rather than be paralyzed by fear.

I managed the delicate moves needed to get us through the hardest part — and three and a half hours later, we were on the top. I was so happy because I felt as if I'd slain a huge dragon! The dragon, of course, was the ugly lie of "I can't." Once I had slain that dragon, it gave me hope that I could tackle other dragons in my life.

Early Morning Climb

For me, the South Col is wind howling like a banshee as it races down the Summit Ridge. This shrieking kept some people awake all night, but I preferred to visualize the wind blowing away my fear and filling me with its energy and strength.

At 2:00 A.M., after just three hours of sleep, the

Summit morning, 7:00 A.M.

TOUGH GOING

Why were we feeling so lousy? The small amount of oxygen in the air is tough on your whole body. Your immune system — it heals your cuts and helps you fight infections — takes a beating. You're not getting the nutritious food you need — it's not available and you're not hungry anyway — and you're sleeping badly, too. On top of that, you're putting out a lot of energy as you push your way up the mountain. No wonder many of us were getting infections and feeling sick.

Sherpas and I got ready to leave Camp Four. At 4:15 A.M., we set off for the summit. Why did we need two hours to prepare to head for the summit? In the thin air near the top of Everest, you don't think straight — your brain doesn't compute things at its normal rate.

Take putting on your footwear — boots first, outer boot shells next, then insulated over-boots and finally crampons. Not complicated, right? At home the whole thing would take five minutes max. At Camp Four it took me more than an hour. Not only was my brain working slowly, my hands were so swollen and infected from cuts that every move was agony.

44

We'd gone the last few days without much sleep, but we all felt okay. Operating mostly on excitement and adrenaline, the three of us drank a cup of hot tea, geared up, roped ourselves together — and were on our way.

It was dark, windy and bitterly cold as we left Camp Four. When we breathed out, our headlamps lit up the ice crystals in our breath. I struggled to stay focused on our goal and thought of the long journey I'd taken to get here. My heart was beating like crazy and I was scared, but I found some peace in moving. It reminded me that when you commit to action, your fear diminishes.

The going was tough at first. Our slow-motion brains made us feel so clumsy that a patch of ice that would normally take 15 minutes to cross took us almost an hour. We had to be careful, but we also had to keep up a good pace. The summit was 900 m (3000 ft.) away, straight up.

The ice climbing technique we used involved flexing our ankles sideways to keep the crampon points in contact with the ice. This cut off blood circulation, and eventually my right foot froze. At one point, we had to stop so I could take off my boot and warm my foot with my bare hands. I re-laced my boot more loosely to improve circulation.

By this time, we were in what climbers call the Death Zone. The oxygen in the air is only one-third what it is at ground level. Your body breaks down and can't heal itself. You don't acclimatize and you don't recuperate.

However slowly our brains were working, they couldn't protect us from the shock of passing the bodies of people who had died in their summit attempts. Most upsetting was a woman who had died on the descent after making it to the summit. She looked as if she'd just dropped off to sleep. Although four other women had successfully climbed Everest by that time, this climber hadn't survived. Sungdare had been with her when she died — I could only imagine how painful it was for him to see her again.

Her corpse reminded me that you are playing for keeps here. Lots of people come this way, but only some return. For Sungdare and Lhakpa Dorje and me, getting to the summit wasn't enough. Success meant coming home alive.

By 8:00 A.M., we'd made it to the South Summit. The weather was clear, but it was freezing and the wind was still howling. The Main Summit — and the most dangerous part of the climb — loomed ahead.

▲ **Our view of the summit as we come around the corner of the ridge.**

Top of the World!

The long ridge between the South and Main Summits is 300 m (985 ft.) of treacherous cornices, overhanging masses of snow that can collapse beneath you at any time. Fall on the south side, and you'd go straight down to Camp Two. Off the north side you'd plummet into Tibet.

Sungdare, Lhakpa Dorje and I shortened the rope between us and agreed that if one fell over the side, the person tied to him would jump off the other side, and the rope would save them both. They'd then climb back up the rope and continue. The alternative of one climber pulling another off the same side of the ridge was far more terrifying.

Quickly, carefully, we climbed in an unchanging routine — dig in the ice ax, take three breaths, then one step, start again.

Just below the sharp ridge to the top is the Hillary Step, a high rock wall. As we scaled the Step, I knew we would make it. I felt I was being lifted by the prayers and wishes of all our friends back in Canada.

At exactly 9:30 A.M., we reached the top. It was October 5, 1982, and I was the 131st person to climb the world's tallest mountain. What a privilege. The world lay spread out below in all directions. We could see forever. It was cramped though — the summit is only as big as a large coffee table.

▲
The Summit Ridge, seen from the Hillary Step.

I shot photo after photo of Sungdare and Lhakpa Dorje and the amazing sights all around me. Then they took photos of me with my other camera. It wasn't until I got back to Canada that I realized the camera had malfunctioned, so there are no photos of me on top of Everest. The only image of me on the summit is in the reflection of Sungdare's and Lhakpa Dorje's sunglasses.

Our Canadian flag was with Kiwi at Camp Three, so I planted my oxygen bottle on the summit. It still held oxygen and had a big happy face drawn on it with a marker. It was better than a flag. It would prove we'd been there, provide oxygen for another climber reaching the top, and leave a Canadian smiling face on the top of the world.

We stayed on top of Everest for 33 minutes — not much, but we
knew that the longer we stayed, the less strength, and oxygen, we
would have. After picking up some rocks from the top and taking one
last, long look, we headed down the Summit Ridge. Eventually I'd feel
a great sense of gratitude, but for now I remained focused on the
immediate details of getting off the mountain alive.

Sungdare and I were moving all right, but Lhakpa Dorje seemed to
run out of energy. Suddenly he collapsed — he had no more oxygen.
Sungdare bravely gave Lhakpa Dorje his bottle and we continued.

After we made it safely off the ridge and were close to the South
Col, Lhakpa Dorje and I plunged into a crevasse. Sungdare held the
rope as we climbed out. But a few steps later, we fell into another
crevasse. Again Sungdare caught us with the rope.

It was noon when we pounded into Camp Four. Dave had tea
waiting. I was so grateful — not only for the tea. It was Dave who
had given me the chance to be the first Canadian on Everest.

There was enough power in the radio to get out a short message.

"Camp Four to Base Camp," I said. "How do you copy?"

"Base Camp to Camp Four. We copy loud and clear."

"Well, copy this!" I shouted. "We did it!!"

In almost no time, all the team members, from Base Camp to
Camp Three, were on the radio, cheering.

**The view from the top
of the world! Far
below is Tibet.**

Dangerous Descent

After a few cups of tea, we got ready to head down. We left all the tents, stoves and sleeping bags for the next group to try reaching the summit.

As we climbed down, we felt better and better. With every step, we were breathing air with more oxygen in it. We reached Camp Two at about 8:00 that night to discover that news of our success had already reached Canada. We'd even received messages of congratulations from our friends back home. In just two days, we'd climbed from Camp Two to the top and back, a

A very happy Pat Morrow (left) and Pema Dorje on the top of Everest. Lhakpa Tshering is reflected in Pema Dorje's glasses.

▼

total of 4900 m (16 000 ft.). No one had ever done that before.

The weather was still good, so Bill decided that Alan, Pat, Pema Dorje Sherpa and Lhakpa Tshering Sherpa should try for the summit. They spent a night at Camp Four and the next morning started out for the summit. We wished them luck.

On the way to the top, Alan's oxygen system malfunctioned. The group tried to fix it in the freezing cold, clinging to the mountain's side, but they couldn't make it work. The Sherpas offered to give Alan one of their oxygen sets and head down, but Alan believed they deserved the summit as much as he did, so he returned to Camp Four. We all felt for him, as he had been on Everest less than a year earlier and had to turn back then, too.

Pat, Pema Dorje and Lhakpa Tshering continued climbing and reached the summit on October 7 at 11:30 A.M. By 6:30 that night, they were back at Camp Two. Pat told me they could still see our footsteps on the Summit Ridge.

The first Canadian Mount Everest Expedition had a lot to be proud of. We'd placed two Canadians and four Sherpas on the summit of Everest, with one-third of our team and one-third of the gear we'd brought. We were lucky that, in one of the stormiest years on record, we had good weather when trying for the summit. I think, though, we created that luck through proper planning, teamwork and commitment.

At the time, I couldn't take it all in. I kept thinking about going through the Icefall, and about our four climbers who had died there. Making it to the top would be a hollow victory if we lost anyone on the descent. Our task was to persist and stay focused until the end. We knew the descent was just as dangerous as the ascent.

The final summit Ridge. Tibet is on the left, Nepal is on the right.

Here we are celebrating in Camp Two.

Heading Home

Pat (right) and I, so happy to have summited and be back in Base Camp.

We carried down as much of our equipment as we could, but we knew we were making only one trip. Since we couldn't carry all the gear, we organized and stored it for a French expedition coming up later that winter.

On October 7, Kiwi, Dave, Dwayne, eight Sherpas and I reached the Icefall — and were greeted by chaos. Ropes had been torn apart, metal ladders were twisted and broken. We repaired them as best and as quickly as we could. But it still took us a whole day to get through the 600 m (2000 ft.) of the Icefall. Then we spread sacred rice as a thank you to the mountain spirits for our safe return.

The next day, Bill, Speedy, Alan, Pat and the remaining Sherpas came down through the Icefall. Pema Dorje, who'd summited with Pat, had become temporarily snow-blind because he'd taken off his goggles on the peak. Bill, carefully guiding him through the Icefall, was the last to descend.

It was so great to get back to Base Camp! For the first time in weeks, we could have a shower. And Canadian newspaper, TV and radio reporters wanted to talk to us. One night, Pat and I spoke on national radio to Canadians via shortwave linked to a satellite dish. It was a great chance to show our appreciation for their support.

After being so cold at the top of Everest, it was wonderful to be back below Base Camp and warm again.

Safe in Base Camp, I finally let myself absorb what we'd accomplished. I'd learned so much. Each lesson remains with me like a road post in my life:

Every great achievement is built on the contributions of many people. Summiting Everest was like a huge gift from many friends, families, Sherpas/Sherpanis, corporate sponsors and the Canadian Everest team members. The goal and the moment belonged to us all.

Confronting and overcoming fear is a choice. You can choose to face fear and take action or to remain paralyzed by it. Backing away from fears makes them seem even bigger! Never say "I can't." By facing fear and taking action, you gain power over it.

Be brave. Sometimes you give a challenging situation your best, but things don't seem to work out the way you'd like them to. All that's left is your courage. Be brave — courage and an honorable goal are undefeatable together.

Finding your uniqueness is a starting point for becoming all you're meant to be. When I was interviewed to join the Everest team, I wasn't asked "Why do you want to go," but "What can you contribute that's uniquely yours?" Finding your uniqueness and using it to help others is something important we all can do.

If you've given more than your best in reaching for a goal, accept whatever level of excellence you're able to achieve. Anything short of "more than your best," and you'll always wonder whether you could've made it. Ever noticed that when a toothpaste tube seems empty, you can still squeeze some more out of it? Reach deep inside for your hidden reserve.

"To serve, to strive and not to yield." Keep this Outward Bound motto in mind when your goals seem out of reach. Often it's the people who persist that prevail over those who may have more talent but give up too soon. Keep at it. Don't yield. Remember, attitude is everything!

Keep your dreams alive. Get committed to your dreams and work toward them!

This was what I was thinking about as I helped the rest of the team pack up. I was the last to leave Base Camp. As I trekked out, I caught sight of stone pillars that had been part of a terrifying nightmare I'd had on our way in. In my dream, I'd seen so many beautiful sights on the walk, but it was a one-way trip — I feared I wouldn't make it out alive.

Seeing those pillars again was overwhelming, and I realized how lucky I was. For Blair Griffiths and Sherpas Ang Chuldim, Dawa Dorje and Pasang Sona, my nightmare had come true. I cried.

▲

Dave Read descending the last section of the Icefall. We were all so relieved to climb through the Icefall for the last time.

Sungdare (left), Lhakpa Dorje and I back in Base Camp after summiting.

▼

Here are the eight of us who were the last to fly home to Canada: (from left to right) me, Alan, Bill, Dave Read, John, Lloyd, Gordon and Dwayne.

◄

After Everest

Today I travel across North America speaking to groups about our Everest climb. Often I imagine seeing the four climbers who died on Everest at the back of an audience. I know they appear to remind me to tell our story with the same passion and conviction we'd all put into that climb.

It was an honor to be on Everest. I'd read and heard so much about the mountain that it had become a powerful symbol to me of giving your absolute best to achieve a difficult goal. I made it to the top because I was willing to give more than my best toward a goal that mattered to me. I wanted to give something back to my country and felt the team could do that if we achieved the summit. I knew we'd touched the heart of our country — the thousands of postcards from people telling us we made them proud to be Canadian told me so.

I also wanted to climb this amazing mountain to see if I had learned anything from being an Outward Bound instructor. Had I truly learned to be part of a team, or was I just good at being a leader? Was I willing to make a real effort, "to serve, to strive and not to yield," as the Outward Bound motto so clearly demands? Everest gave me positive answers to all these questions and much more.

The first two Canadians to climb Mount Everest back in Calgary.

Since 1982, I've been back to Everest a number of times. In 1986, I returned with a small team, using less gear and funded with much less money. The expedition was called Everest Light, and our route was a lot more difficult than the one we'd taken in 1982. So we were very proud when, on May 20, 1986, Canadians Dwayne Congdon and Sharon Wood climbed to the summit.

Sharon Wood carrying a heavy load on Everest in 1986.

Sharon was the first woman from the Western Hemisphere to summit Everest — the sixth woman ever to stand on top of the world.

We were pleased that no one in the Everest Light team died, no one was injured, and we left the mountain cleaner than we found it. Women like Sharon are tremendous role models for my daughter Natasha's generation.

Today, I'm still involved with Outward Bound and continue to climb in the Himalayas, Andes and throughout North America. My favorite climb, and one close to my heart, happened when the principal of a local school in Calgary invited me to talk to his students about Everest. Afterward, some of the kids asked me to take them up a mountain. I agreed and organized two trips to nearby Mount Yamnuska.

Coincidentally, this same principal's father had buried my beloved mother when I was trapped on a mountain and unable to be at her funeral service. I knew this would be a powerful climb for us all.

Natasha — she was 8 — and another girl, Vicky, assisted me as guides on the two climbs to the 2290 m (7500 ft.) mountain summit. These girls showed such fine leadership qualities that the climb was profiled on the front page of a Calgary newspaper and shown on TV across Canada.

We're all climbers at heart, with mountains we're trying to climb or goals we're trying to achieve, goals that are right for each of us. Remember, being defeated is often a temporary condition — giving up is what makes it permanent.

So what are your dreams? Are you willing to try to achieve them? Whether you achieve them or not, you succeed when you try more than your best!

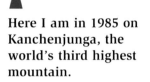

Here I am in 1985 on Kanchenjunga, the world's third highest mountain.

Today I guide mostly in Canada and Argentina, where we climb the Western Hemisphere's highest mountain, Nevado Aconcagua.

Glossary

altitude sickness: Illness climbers can get when they climb above 3050 m (10 000 ft.). It's caused by the decrease of oxygen in the atmosphere.

Base Camp: Main camp on the edge of the glacier at the base of Everest, at 5200 m (17 000 ft.)

carabiner: Metal link that attaches two things together, such as a climber to a rope or anchor. It can hold up to 2270 kg (5000 lb.).

Col: Welsh word for saddle or pass. The South Col was the site of Camp Four. It is between Everest and Lhotse, at 7920 m (26 000 ft.).

cornice: Frozen wave of hardened snow along a ridge, formed by wind

crampons: Spiked steel framework that's attached to the bottom of a boot. It gives a climber grip when moving on ice and snow.

crevasse: Deep, long, narrow crack in the ice of a glacier

Cwm: Welsh word for valley. The Western Cwm lies between the west ridge of Everest and the west ridge of Nuptse.

fix rope: To attach rope to a mountainside, using snow, ice and rock anchors

Geneva Spur: Black ridge of rock that starts at about 7320 m (24 000 ft.). It is the last major obstacle before reaching the last camp on Everest.

Hillary Step: The last obstacle before Everest's summit. It lies at about 8760 m (28 750 ft.) and is a 12 m (40 ft.) high rock cliff along the Summit Ridge.

ice axe: Tool used by mountain climbers to climb steep, snowy mountains or cliffs. It can be used to hook or cut holes in the snow and ice.

ice screw: One of the main types of anchors used for climbing ice. This hollow steel tube is screwed into hard ice and a climber clips her rope into the screw with a carabiner.

Lhotse: Mountain just south of Everest. Its name is Tibetan for "South Peak." Lhotse is 8510 m (27 920 ft.) high, the world's fourth highest mountain.

merchant seaman: Sailor who works on commercial (not defense) ships

Nuptse: Mountain near Everest. Its name is Tibetan for "Peak to the West of Everest." Nuptse is 7880 m (25 850 ft.) high, the world's 26th highest mountain.

Petzl ascender: Mechanical device that climbers attach to a rope. It slides in one direction and locks in the other and so protects climbers while they're moving on fixed rope.

rappel: To slide down a fixed rope that has been clipped through a device attached to a climber. The rappel device allows the climber to control her descent.

snow fluke: Flat, metal snow anchor shaped like a pointed shovel blade. It is pounded into or buried in snow. Snow flukes hold well in soft, deep snow.

snow picket: Long, aluminum anchor hammered into hard snow to fix ropes

Summit Ridge: A crest of snow leading up to the highest point on Everest. It's about 150 m (500 ft.) long, at a height of 8800–8850 m (28 870–29 030 ft.).

Check out **www.skresletadventureservices.com** to find out more about Laurie.